To My Grandchildren, My Inspiration.
- Giddo M.

Text Copyright © 2022 by Mohamed El Mouelhi.
Illustrations Copyright © 2022 by Hossam El Mouelhi and Donia Farouk.

All Rights Reserved. No part of this book may be reproduced, transmitted, or stored in an information retrieval system in any form or by any means, graphic, electronic, or mechanical, including photocopying, taping, and recording, without prior written permission from the publisher.

جميع الحقوق محفوظة.

ISBN 978-1-7357701-8-5

First edition 2022

Published by Honey Elm Books LLC
www.HoneyElmBooks.com

Nuh (Noah) PBUH
نوح عليه السلام

Editing: Noha Elmouelhi

Artistic Preparation: Hossam El Mouelhi - Donia Farouk

تحرير: نهى المويلحي

الإعداد الفني: حسام المويلحي – دنيا فاروق

Several generations after Prophet Adam, there was a group of people living in Asia. Among them were righteous people who used to do good. But after some time, their people began building statues of them to honor them and then began to worship those statues. Allah sent them a prophet from among them - Prophet Nuh - to guide them back to the worship of Allah.

جاءت مجموعة من الناس في منطقة آسيا بعد عدة أجيال من آدم عليه السلام، وكان من بينهم أشخاص أتقياء فاعلين للخير، وبعد فترة من الزمان أقام لهم الناس تماثيلاً لتكريمهم. ولكن الناس أتجهوا لعبادة هذه التماثيل، فأرسل الله لهم نبياً من بينهم – نوح – لدعوتهم الى عبادة الله وحده.

Nuh was a righteous man
and didn't believe in worshiping idols.
So, Allah chose him to call his people
to worship Allah - the only God Who can benefit
or harm anyone.
Only a few people followed Nuh
and believed his message.

وكان نوح رجلاً صالحاً ولا يعتقد فى عبادة التماثيل، وقد اختاره الله ليدعو قومه الى عبادة الله وحده الذى ينفع ويضر من يشاء. وآمن بنوح عدد قليل من قومه.

The leaders of his people didn't believe him as he was just an ordinary person; he was not wealthy or powerful. The non-believers called Nuh and his followers liars. Nuh advised them to believe in Allah before Allah punishes them.

ولكن زعماء قومه كفروا بدعوته لأنه كان بشراً عادياً مثلهم وليس مَلَكاً أو شخصاً غنياً ذا نفوذ، فاتّهموا نوح والذين آمنوا به بالكذب، فنصحهم نوح بالإيمان بالله قبل أن يوقع الله بهم عذابه.

Nuh didn't give up and continued calling his people to worship only Allah for many years. They laughed at Allah's torment to the extent they asked Nuh to have Allah's punishment be inflicted on them.

He answered them saying that only Allah is capable of bringing His torment on whom He wants and when He decides; at that moment there will be no escape.

ولم ييأس نوح وأستمر في دعوة قومه للإيمان بالله لعدة أعوام طويلة، ولكنهم إستهزؤوا به وسخروا من عذاب الله حتى طلبوا من نوح أن ينزل ربه بهم عذابه. فرد عليهم أن الله وحده هو الذى يستطيع أن ينزل عذابه على من يشاء وحين يشاء، وحينها فلن يستطيعوا النجاة منه.

At this stage,
Allah ordered Nuh to build a large ship.
His people made more fun of him for building
an ark on land so far away from the sea.
Allah then informed Nuh that He will destroy all
the non-believers and drown them.
Nuh felt sorry for his people as they were his relatives and
friends.
But this was Allah's decree and punishment for their disbelief.

وبعدها أمر الله نوح أن يقوم ببناء سفينة كبيرة، ولما رأى قومه بناءه لسفينة كبيرة بعيداً عن البحر إستهزؤا به وظنوا أنه مجنون.

وشعر نوح بالأسف تجاه قومه عندما أخبره الله أنه سيغرقهم جميعاً جزاءً لكفرهم وشركهم إلا من آمن به.

وحزن نوح لما سيحل بقومه وأقاربه، ولكن كان هذا أمر الله وعقابه لهم.

After Nuh
finished building the ark,
Allah ordered him to bring onto the ship
with him all the believers and a pair of all animals
(a male and female) to be saved.
All the non-believers would be left behind.
Then, Allah's command came to flood all the land.
Heavy rains covered all the land, and the people
who were left behind perished in the flood.

وبعد أن أنتهى نوح من بناء السفينة أمره الله أن يحمل فيها من كل كائن حي زوجين (ذكر وأنثى)، وكذلك من آمن من أهله وقومه وأن يترك من كفر منهم.
بعد ذلك جاء أمر الله بالفيضان وغمرت المياه سطح الأرض وغرق كل من بقى عليها.

" ... We said: `Embark therein,
of each kind a pair,
and your family - except those against whom
the word has already gone forth-,
and the believers ... ' "(Hud: 40)

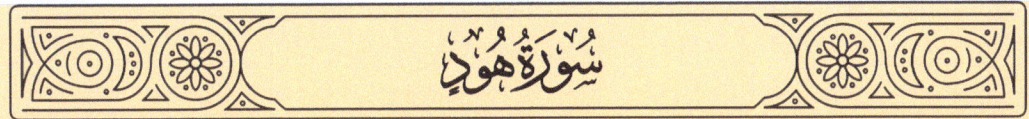

بِسْمِ اللَّهِ الرَّحْمَٰنِ الرَّحِيمِ

... قُلْنَا ٱحْمِلْ فِيهَا مِن كُلٍّ زَوْجَيْنِ ٱثْنَيْنِ وَأَهْلَكَ إِلَّا مَن سَبَقَ عَلَيْهِ ٱلْقَوْلُ وَمَنْ ءَامَنَ ... ﴿٤٠﴾

The big ship sailed above the high waves protected by Allah. As Nuh watched the land get flooded around him, he saw his son still on land and about to drown. Nuh asked his son to embark with them, but his son said he will take refuge on a big mountain that will protect him from the flood.

وأبحرت السفينة وسط الأمواج العالية بإذن الله ومشيئته، وغمر الماء كل شئ على وجه الأرض، وقد رأى نوح إبنه وهو يصارع الأمواج وكان على وشك الغرق، فقال لإبنه: يا بنى أركب معنا فى السفينة، فرد عليه إبنه أنه سيذهب الى جبل عالي ويحتمى به من الماء المندفع.

Nuh told his son
that there is no shelter from
Allah's command except to believe in Allah
and His power.
The son was stubborn, insisted on refusing any help
from his father, and was among those who drowned.
This was a very difficult scene for a loving father
to witness his own son refusing help
and drowning before him.

فقال له نوح أن اليوم لا عاصم من أمر الله، وأن النجاة تكون فقط بالإيمان بالله وقدرته، ولكن إبن نوح أصر على عناده، فكان من المغرقين، وكان هذا موقفاً صعباً على نوح وهو يرى إبنه الذى يحبه يغرق.

Nuh was so concerned
and asked Allah why his son had
not been saved.
Allah told Nuh that his son had not believed
in the One, True Message and those who continued
to deny the Message were punished in the flood.

وحين ذاك دعا نوح ربه مستوضحاً لماذا أُغرِق إبنه الذى هو من أهله، فقال له الله أنه من الذين كفروا بالله ، وبناءً عليه فهَو ليس من أهل نوح، إنما هو من الكافرين المغرقين الذين يستحقون عذاب الله.

This was a special divine
teaching from Allah to His prophet
to not ask about matters that he has
no knowledge about.
Allah is The All-Knower.
Nuh asked Allah to forgive him for inquiring about what
he was not aware of.

وعلّم الله نبيه أنه لا يحق أن يسأل ما ليس له به علم، وأن الله وحده هو العليم بكل شيء، وحينها أستغفر نوح ربه على أنه سأله ما ليس له به علم.

"He said: `O my Lord!
I seek refuge with You from asking
You that of which I have no knowledge.
And unless You forgive me and have Mercy on me,
I will indeed be one of the losers.'"
(Hud: 47)

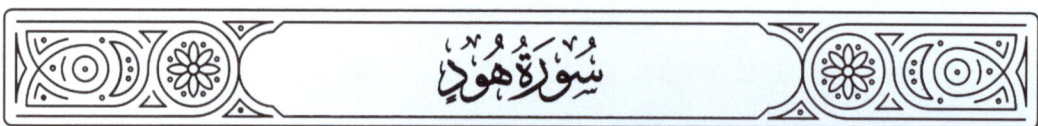

بِسْمِ اللَّهِ الرَّحْمَٰنِ الرَّحِيمِ

قَالَ رَبِّ إِنِّي أَعُوذُ بِكَ أَنْ أَسْأَلَكَ مَا لَيْسَ لِي بِهِ عِلْمٌ وَإِلَّا تَغْفِرْ لِي وَتَرْحَمْنِي أَكُن مِّنَ الْخَاسِرِينَ ﴿٤٧﴾

After all the land
had been flooded and all the
non-believers had perished, Allah ordered
the rain to stop and the land
to swallow up the water.
The blessed ship landed safely on a high mountain
and all its passengers were saved from Allah's torment and
punishment because they had believed
in Allah's oneness and power.

وبعد أن غمر الماء المنهمر كل ما على الأرض وغرق كل من لم يؤمن بالله، أمر الله السماء أن يتوقف نزول الماء الغزير منها، وأن تبتلع الأرض الماء الكثيف الذى عليها، وأمر الله أن ترسى السفينة على جبل عالي، ونجا بها كل من آمن بالله.

"And it was said: `O earth! Swallow up your water, and O sky! Withhold (your rain).' And the water was made to subside and the Decree of Allah was fulfilled. And the ship rested on Mount Judi, and it was said: `Away with the people who are wrong-doers!' " (Hud: 44)

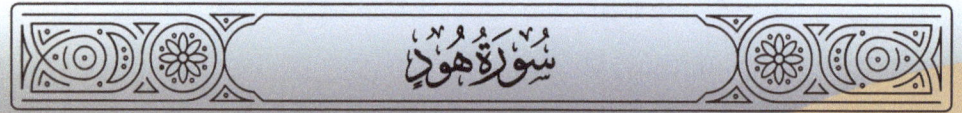

بِسْمِ ٱللَّهِ ٱلرَّحْمَٰنِ ٱلرَّحِيمِ

وَقِيلَ يَٰأَرْضُ ٱبْلَعِي مَآءَكِ وَيَٰسَمَآءُ أَقْلِعِي وَغِيضَ ٱلْمَآءُ وَقُضِيَ ٱلْأَمْرُ وَٱسْتَوَتْ عَلَى ٱلْجُودِيِّ وَقِيلَ بُعْدًا لِّلْقَوْمِ ٱلظَّٰلِمِينَ ۝

Nuh and the passengers
of the ship disembarked from the ark,
and began to rebuild their lives from anew.
With this restart of civilization,
Prophet Nuh is also considered to be
the Father of Humanity after Prophet Adam.

ونزل نوح ومن معه من المؤمنين من السفينة وبدأوا عمارة الأرض من جديد. ويُعتبر نوح أبو البشرية بعد آدم عليهما السلام.

NUH'S STORY HAS MANY IMPORTANT LESSONS FOR US TO REMEMBER:

-Don't judge others because of their wealth, social status, or belief.

-Respect others, especially those who do good deeds.

-Be honest with your parents and listen to them. They truly care about you.

-We have limited knowledge as humans, and we should always trust in what Allah has told us or ordained for us.

فى قصة سيدنا نوح عدة دروس هامة منها:

– عدم الحكم على الآخرين تبعاً لدرجة الغنى أو الوضع الإجتماعي أو العقيدة.

-إحترام الآخرين وخاصة الصالحين منهم.

-ضرورة الصدق وطاعة الوالدين فهما أكثر من يحبون الخير لأولادهم.

– التعرف على قدراتنا ومعرفتنا وإتباع أوامر الله لنا.

Watch a special reading of Nuh PBUH by the author!

Scan this QR code to access the video.

www.ingramcontent.com/pod-product-compliance
Lightning Source LLC
Chambersburg PA
CBHW040024130526
44590CB00036B/81